In a Class of Their Own

The Power of Mentorship for African American Women in Leadership

Dr. Brenda J. Walker

Published by So It Is Written, LLC
Detroit, MI
SoItIsWritten.net

In a Class of Their Own: The Power of Mentorship for African American Women in Leadership
Copyright © 2021 by Dr. Brenda J. Walker

Edit by: So It Is Written – www.SoItIsWritten.net

Formatting: Ya Ya Ya Creative – www.yayayacreative.com

ISBN: 978-1-7362170-7-8

LCCN: 2021901234

PRINTED AND BOUND IN THE UNITED STATES OF AMERICA

Praise for
In a Class of Their Own

"Marginalized, overlooked, insignificant. Those are words that in times past have incorrectly described the role of African American women in our society. If we add sexism and racism to the problem, there seems to be no way out. But most notably, in the first two decades of the 21st century, those words have faded significantly as Black women rise from obscurity to top positions in all industries of our society.

In her book, Dr. Brenda J. Walker celebrates the rise of African American women, as she details the struggles they have endured. Brilliantly, Dr. Walker uses the simplicity and complexity of a quilt and the various patches that make it up to understand African American women. She offers mentoring as therapy for uncovering the hidden or suppressed abilities in African American women. Quotes from scholars past and present, along with confirmed research, makes her book stand out from other so-called books on solutions for African Americans. Indeed, she has combined her own expertise with that of accredited others to provide real, lasting solutions to an age-old issue. This book is truly a great investment!"

Gail Perry-Mason
Author, *Girl Make Your Money Grow!*

❦

"In today's corporate world, white men make up over 72% of Fortune 500 companies' senior executives. Corporate America can be a white male dominated world, full of blatant racism and sexism that is impossible to avoid. In this book, Dr. Walker reiterates the importance of Black women gaining knowledge and wisdom to excel in leadership roles. In addition, she further proves that having a Black woman with leadership experience maneuvering through the corporate environment is invaluable for so many reasons."

Jermaine Johnson
CEO, *Jerm Consulting*

❦

"Dr. Brenda J. Walker has developed an excellent resource for Black women that you'll want to share with every woman in your life! This book teaches women how to break through many of the common barriers Black women face in leadership and provides practical guidance that is helpful at every level of your career."

Racheal Allen
Chief Operating Officer, *Marygrove Conservancy*

Acknowledgments

Proverbs 3:6 says, *In all your ways acknowledge Him, And He shall direct your paths.* I want to thank my personal Savior, the Lord Jesus Christ. It is because of Him that I live, breathe and have my being. He has also made me realize that I can do all things through Christ, who strengthens me (Philippians 4:13).

I would like to thank my parents, the late Leroy and Rosa Walker, for their love and support. I now recognize the sacrifices you both have made so that my siblings and I could have a better life. I love you both and appreciate you very much. I know, many times, they did not understand my motivation, but still gave me all their support. Thank you for your unconditional love. I am thankful for the love of my number one fan, my son, Avery Exum Walker, and my daughter-in-law, Nicole. To Ava and Raina, the two newest loves of my life. Gia loves you both and look forward to sharing in who you become.

I acknowledge and thank my sisters, their mates and their children. The Washingtons: Rene', Thomas, Corey, Arria and Adrienne; The Aversas: Sonja, Nicholas, Pauly and Sam; The Amicas: Pearlene, Willis, Will and Christian; The Christies: Melissa, Rueben, Amaya, R.J. and Preston. To my brothers, their mates and their children: The Walkers: Lorenzo, Cindy, Dwayne, Lorae and Lorenzo. To my newest heartthrob, Zaire. The Marshalls: Roy Lee, Brenda, Roy, Jr., Chontelle Forrest and Shoyja. You all have been great.

To the memory of my late Grandma Liz (Elizabeth Shine), a pillar of strength. Your words of encouragement and spirit will stay with me for life. To the memory of my paternal grandmother, the late Minnie Lee Jordan Walker and my aunts, the late Pearlie May Byrd, the late Augusta Flucker. Three more examples of the strong women in the family that have gone on. May their strength continue throughout the rest of the female members of the family. You have been great role models and mentors. To my aunts Christine Brown and Fannye Lou Walker, thank you for being there as I grew into a young lady. To Cynthia Byrd: Thank you for your encouragement and excitement about this project. You have been a blessing!

To the rest of my extended Walker family, I appreciate you all.

To my church family: You all have helped to make this all possible. To Elder Kenneth and Sandra Reed for your prayers and support. To Mother Beatrice Matthews for your loving words of kindness throughout my life. To the late Mother Essie Mae Hall, I appreciate and cherish the time we spent together, talking and enjoying each other. You will be greatly missed. To the entire Greater Evangelical family: I love and appreciate you all. To my One Touch Ministries family: Thank you. To Mother Lavern Knowles: I appreciate you so.

To my close friends: Milly Marion James, Laurita Washington, Lee Singleton, Sherita Knowles, Jacquelyn Bolden, Loretta Herring, Angela Rogers, Jonquil Terry, Janice Johnson, Tenita Johnson, Goldie Holmes, Regeina Braden, Brenda Dilworth, Lisa Kirkendolph. Thanks for being a sounding board and for being there when I needed you most. To Paula Lampley, also a close and dear friend who has really helped me: I thank you for being there then and now. Our friendship endured the thirty-five months and the struggles we had along the journey, which made us the strong women we are today. Thanks for being there when I felt as if I could not go any further and wanted to throw in the towel. I appreciate you. I am glad we met and became and stayed friends until this very day. I love you, my sister. Thanks for the sisterhood, Dr. Paula Lampley.

To God be the glory for the things He has done.

"Here's to good women.
May we know them.
May we be them.
May we raise them."
−UNKNOWN

Foreword

W hat's that word … help me, queens. You know the word. It's when you feel immediate ease because it seems as if a perfect stranger has walked a mile in your stilettos. Or she has been in step with you as you trudged through the battleground of life/work/home *imbalance* with your cape tucked into your waistband. That word is "kindred" and let me just say that Dr. Brenda Walker (aka "I am Brenda") has been that to me. How fitting that my mentor, Dr. Lisa J.L. Wicker, Founder of *Career Mastered Magazine*, thought to introduce me to Brenda. You see, mentoring, when done to "create" for ourselves, and activated as an extension of our collective vocations it manages to maximize influence, sponsorship and advocacy on your behalf.

In 2018, I retired at age 41 from a male-dominated law enforcement career, in part, to actively be about the business of influencing the people behind their brands. I call that a win. In the pages that you'll read next, Brenda delivers a declaration for times such as these. The time for accepting invisibility on your job, in your community and at home has expired. It's game time and Dr. Walker is the coach, training our squad on how to run up the scoreboard. Her expertise in Organizational Leadership, her brilliance in developing mentoring programs, and her vivid successes and shifts in behavior, even when mentored from afar, will boost you into a winning position.

Our future depends on your successes. The race to the future will be won by determination, purpose, creativity, faith and creating modern mentoring programs that unify us and actually meet our needs and desires. Representation matters. Brenda gets that. Yes, we *can* be matched to a mentor at work or in the business community. *However*, wouldn't it just be great to see our cream rise to the top of a group of Black women mentors to select from? Rise, queens. We are kindred spirits and forward-thinkers. We are beyond due respect *and* our time is now. That's the vibe that I get from this book. I think you will, too.

We've seen the barriers keeping our greatness at bay, dimming our light. And can we be honest, sis? Just between us, sometimes the barrier is "me, I, us, we." Brenda's words will work that out, though. If you're reading this far, I sense that you're looking for that kindred, familiar representative, and likewise, looking to improve the narrative that you tell yourself. Well, I declare that I cannot keep Dr. Brenda Walker a secret. By the time you've flipped these pages to the back cover, you'll be running down the field, scoring goals and finding wins in your next mentoring relationships. Dare I say, you'll be the queen mentioning others' names in rooms full of opportunities. Let's go, team!

Cheering for you,

Tisha Hammond

International Bestselling Author, *Daily Devotional for Entrepreneurs: Your Season to Grow*

Copy Editor, *Career Mastered Magazine*

Introduction

⎯⎯⎯⎯⎯⎯ ⟨⟩⟨⟩⟨⟩ ⎯⎯⎯⎯⎯⎯

Many people who have experienced being mentored recognize that something incredibly special has happened, but they may not have known what to call the experience (Shea, 2002). Often, a mentoring program is a process whereby the mentor and mentee work together to discover and develop the mentee's latent abilities, provide the mentee with knowledge and skills, and serve as a tutor, counselor and friend to the mentee (Shea, 2002).

A growing number of scholars have recognized that women seeking to enter mentoring relationships face a myriad of challenges and obstacles as a result of gender biases (Blake, 1998). A body of literature has developed this premise and addresses the concerns of women in the mentoring process (Clawson & Kram, 1984; Collins, 1983; Fitt & Newton, 1981; Halcomb, 1980; Nieva & Gutek, 1981; Noe, 1986; Ragins, 1989; Blake, 1998). Blake (1998) indicated that the voices of African American women are still unheard, and this silence gives cause for the need to have a mentoring program for African American women.

In today's workplace, African American women may feel alone or isolated from the mainstream of women and the mentoring relationships in the organization (Duff, 1999). African American women are many times overlooked, or not considered to participate in these relationships that would lend to one successfully navigating the organization. Catalyst, a New York based organization promoting women in executive positions, reported that of the 57.8 million women in the workforce, 23% are minorities. However, African American women make up only 14% of the 2.9 million women in managerial positions (Cuff, 1999). Finding a mentor of the same race or ethnicity may be a difficult challenge for African American women in corporate America. Often, African American women have no contact with other African American women in the workplace because many organizations have a predominately white workplace culture.

Beale (1979) coined the term double jeopardy to describe the dual discrimination of racism and sexism facing African American women. Nkomo (1988) stated, "African American women must constantly battle the assumption that they are both racially and sexually inferior" (p. 137). Essed (1991) noted that the inability to separate the specific impact of either race or gender leads to a form of gendered racism that supports the experience of African American women. These assumptions of African American women being racially and sexually inferior is just that: *an assumption*. This again speaks to the importance of African American women working with other African American female mentors in the corporate space. This is an opportunity for Black women to learn from each other and have candid conversations of what is taking place in the lives of Black women.

Increased support systems, such as mentoring programs, may help raise the self-esteem level of African American women and have a lifelong positive effect on their lives.

DuBois (1903) wrote about the *Negro* as being a sort of seventh son, born with a veil, and gifted with second sight in this American world, a world that yields him no true self-consciousness, but only lets him see himself through the revelation of the other world. He identified this peculiar sensation, as double consciousness:

> A sense of always looking at one's self through the eyes of others, of measuring one's soul by the tape of a world that looks on in amused contempt and pity. One ever feels his twoness, An American, a Negro; two souls, two thoughts, two unreconciled strivings;

two warring ideals in one dark body, whose dogged strength alone keeps it from being torn asunder.

DuBois published this statement in the early 19th century to describe the African American experience of living in America, a society based largely on denial of respect and full rights to African Americans (Blake, 1998). Although this statement is dated to the early 19th century, it is relevant to many of the experiences that African Americans face in America today. The double consciousness that DuBois described is currently defined as biculturalism, or living in two worlds (Blake, 1998). Blake (1998) believed that DuBois' statement is particularly descriptive of the corporate experience of African Americans.

A second and third generation of African American college graduates have graduated from America's universities and gone to corporate America to reap the benefits of their education, such as cars, houses in suburbia, vacations, expensive clothes and jewelry, and electronic gadgets. Yet, the mantle of education, oftentimes earned at elite universities, is not enough to ward off the harsh effects of racism (Blake, 1998). Differences between African Americans and Whites in terms of income, ability to be promoted, satisfaction, and other organizational outcomes are well documented (Braddock & McPartland, 1987; Cox

& Nkomo, 1991; Davis & Watson, 1982; Fernandez, 1981; Blake, 1998). Even if a variety of factors, such as education, socioeconomic status, age and background are held constant, research shows that African Americans are still fighting to gain equality with Whites in the corporate sector (Blake, 1998).

African Americans are pulled to succeed in the predominately White corporate sector; yet, they are drawn to the African American community (Blake, 1998). By necessity, African Americans are often bicultural, moving back and forth between their predominantly white professional spheres and the African American community (Bell, 1990; Blake, 1998). Blake (1998) believed that although African American men and women face the effects of racism and the stress of being bicultural, African American women are in an even more tenuous position within the labor market.

In American history, institutional racism has had a major impact on the development of African American self-esteem and group identity (Allen, 2001). African Americans have developed strong tenacious concepts of self, partially based on the (a) African culture, (b) philosophical retention, and (c) as a reaction to the historical injustices (Allen, 2001). African Americans reside in a society that expects them to adhere to the values, culture and beliefs of European Americans.

Sexism and racism have contributed to African American women's dismal experiences in history (Neville & Hamler, 2000). Hooks (1989) found that, "When I began the long search in history, sociology, and psychology texts for material, I was surprised that African American women were rarely a category in anyone's index, that when we were written about, we rarely rated more than a few sentences or paragraphs". Too often, it is assumed that through a study of African American males, African American women are better understood. Alternatively, studies of White women are assumed to encompass the experiences of their African American counterparts (Blake, 1998). Both assumptions are erroneous and detrimental; both assumptions render African American women invisible (King, 1998).

The experiences of African American women have been largely neglected as a focus for social science research (Graham, 1992; Reid & Kelly, 1994; Thomas & Miles, 1995; Blake, 1998). The challenges facing African American women can be seen as not just filling a void, but as adding more patches to an ever-evolving quilt. The image of the quilt, and the patches added, have contributed more texture and depth to the understanding of African American women (Bond, 1997). We can be enriched by exploring the unique pattern of each patch. It is this diversity, among the patches, that provides the answers to the questions—questions that serve as the threads that hold the quilt together. Identification of the questions is a critical step regarding research on African American women. Once the issues that impact African American women are identified, we can increase our understanding of their challenges and work to address solutions.

Table of Contents

CHAPTER 1

Corporate America's Misunderstanding of Mentorship for the Black Woman

It was a normal busy Thursday afternoon before our quarterly town hall meeting. I'd just come back into my office from speaking with an employee. I felt the need to share my findings with the site manager about the employee's concerns.

"Shawn, I was out and about outside the main building. John stopped me and asked me about his 401k. I told him I could give him information, but that he should probably talk to Susan since I'm no longer in that role."

He immediately stopped me mid-sentence.

"You are no longer in that role!" he yelled. "You need to focus on the role that you're currently in. If you're having a problem with that, then maybe we should sit down and discuss it."

He said this in front of a senior leader whom he was grooming to take over his role. To say the least, I was embarrassed and left speechless. I sat down and waited for his cue to start the town hall. While waiting for the meeting to begin, my heart beat faster as I was in disbelief that this was even happening. When I did start the meeting, I felt like I was just going through the motions. My heart wasn't in it.

What had just happened?

Why had it happened?

And, more importantly, what do I need to do to make it stop?

Two days later, Shawn approached me and joked about our previous conversation.

"What was the employee asking you, and what did you tell him?" he asked.

"I told the employee that he would need to contact the person who is currently in the role. He tried contacting Susan, but she was unresponsive."

Then Shawn said, "Yeah, I'll look into that because every employee needs to feel valued. And if he doesn't feel valued, that's a problem."

I thought to myself, *Why couldn't he simply have addressed the question then with the conversation we had today? Why did he feel the need to embarrass me in front of another male senior leader versus hearing my thoughts out? And what about my value? Shouldn't I matter, too?*

As time progressed, occurrences like played out before my very eyes over and over again. Before long, he was having a conversation with me about my position being eliminated because of a merger in September of 2014. He offered me a demotion or a severance package, which meant I would have had to start over somewhere else. He advised me to seek legal counsel and let him know my decision. Between September and the end of the year, I was responsible for hosting the company's open house, the annual company holiday party and the grand opening for a new building onsite. Little did I know, my end was near. Shawn had made no additional comments or moves to signal to me that my position was still being eliminated.

In January of 2015, Shawn asked me to provide the goals and objectives for a management job I would ideally take over should I have decided to be demoted. The next day, I had to meet with the senior vice president of HR from the corporate office. There was no discussion of any demotion or job move. I was presented with a severance package letter and told to vacate the premises *immediately*. I went back to my office, packed my desk, and put my things in my car. The next day, Shawn called me and acted as if he was unaware of what had happened the day before.

"When you didn't show up at today's team meeting, I was wondering what happened! I didn't realize this was coming. I can't believe they would do this to you."

"Well, you're the general manager. Aren't you?" I asked him. "Don't you have a say so in what happens?"

"Brenda, I had no idea. If you're willing, we can meet downtown for lunch and discuss it further."

I declined lunch with Shawn and never heard from him again.

Unfortunately, for many Black women in corporate America, this story is all too familiar. It's more common than many companies would like to admit, and it's more common than Black women in the corporate world would like to report. In many arenas, White men are the only available mentors for all groups of employees, including Black women. Many times, those men don't value the skills Black women bring to the table, and even when they do, they discount it or they take credit for the work Black women have done. It's also frustrating to know that, as a member of the senior leadership team, I performed much more work than my colleagues, but was paid much less than them. Many of the White males who were my senior counterparts made $30K, $40K or even $50K more than me. Because I worked in HR, I knew the salaries of all employees. So, there it was for me, in black and white—*literally*.

The premise of this book is to solely highlight the disadvantages of Black women not having similar role models to follow when they're placed in leadership positions. Many times, if there hasn't been a Black woman who has come before us in a certain role, we don't know the pitfalls or the land mines to avoid. We are not always invited to golf outings or happy hours at the bar after work. Even when African American women are included in those groups, they're given a seat at the table for ulterior motives, not to have their voices heard sincerely at the table.

African American women have limited opportunities to interact with other African American women in the workplace due to the lack of African American women in managerial positions (Duff, 1999). As a result, African American women often lack mentoring relationships with members of their own race and gender. In this book, we will explore how mentoring programs impact self-esteem and ability among African American women in leadership, as well as the responsibility one holds for the generation of leaders coming behind her. I strongly believe that we can transform the landscape of corporate America through the use of mentee/mentor relationships across all industries, positioning Black women worldwide to successfully compete with their male and female White counterparts.

Mentoring

More often than not, African American women in leadership are mentored by their White male counterparts. The number of women and minorities in high-level corporate positions who have served as mentors is limited (Ibarra, 1993; Duff, 1999). Thomas (1990), in his study of race and mentoring relationships, found African Americans in upper-level positions comprised less than 5% of the total number of professionals in the stratum and that White men predominately served as mentors to all four race-gender groups he studied: White men, African American men, African American women and White women.

In terms of sisterhood, it would seem that African American women would gain their greatest support from White women. This did not prove to be so. Blake (1998) found that African American women overwhelmingly expressed feelings of anger and distrust toward White women. This legacy of anger, mistrust and fear of betrayal has important implications for the relationships, mentoring as well as others, in which African American women and White women can engage. Thomas (1990) described the female-female cross-race relationship using the analogy of African American women as the house slave and the White women as the mistress in the historical context. Because of the "congenial and supportive nature" of this relationship, Thomas (1990) suggested that African American and White women are not able to interact in a manner that suppresses their racial difference to draw upon their shared womanhood. This bond of womanhood does not overcome the racial differences (Duff, 1999).

The organizational mentoring experiences of women, particularly African American women, are an important and growing area of study (Blake, 1998). Mentoring, in the classical sense, can be used as a beacon in the rough terrain of the corporate sector (Blake, 1998). Blake (1998) believed that mentoring could serve to illuminate the path, which has been obscured by the soil of the historical relationship between African American women and White women. Mentoring provides the necessary cues to climb the corporate ladder. Where the slippery spots are, mentoring can serve to illuminate the way for those that follow (Blake, 1998).

Self-Esteem

Self-esteem is a construct that has been studied in several ways: self-concept, self-regard, self-love, self-confidence, sense of competence, ego, and others (Campbell, 1984; Mruk, 1999). Limited research, however, has been conducted on the self-esteem of African Americans. Some of the research that has been conducted concerning African American women has discussed levels of income and education, weight concerns, negative stereotypes, and cost of living, gender and ethnic differences.

Today, the field of research on self-esteem needs to take steps forward. The task is to combat the disparateness of the literature, where much of the research has been carried on in analytical and empirical isolation, and cross-comparisons are difficult (Wells & Maxwell, 1976; Duff, 1999).

Career Advancement

Career advancement and leadership development for African American women should be based on the empowerment model. According to Fong & Furuto (2001), empowerment involves helping people "to discover and use the resources within and around them, and to seize some control over their lives and the decisions that are critical to their lives" (p. 230). They further asserted that to be empowered, a woman needs a nurturing environment that gives her viable options to make choices about her career (Fung & Furuto, 2001). Empowered women, Collins (2000) maintained, assume authority to select from among those options and as Gutierrez (1990) noted, the more options women have for developing their skills and abilities, the greater their sense of empowerment. To this end, Green (2001) believed that African American women mentors and mentees need to work toward developing a more positive and potent sense of self and personal power by showing them how to take risks, link personal and political power, recognize and build on existing strengths, and create a support network; attain the knowledge and skills needed for a more critical comprehension of the social, political and economic realities and constraints of the workplace environment; and make use of resources and specific strategies to attain personal career goals and the collective goal of improving the workplace of others.

Mentoring and Leadership

Mentoring programs can have leadership significance for African American women because most African American women need someone to help navigate various obstacles and teach them the subtle aspects of the work environment

(Bowman, et al., 1998). African American women need guidance in career development to succeed.

In organizations today, mentors serve as leaders. Mentors tend to be the senior people in organizations that work with talented young people to protect, teach, and in some cases, sponsor these mentees (Shea, 2002). Organizations have formal mentoring relationships that are designated by the organization as a voluntary activity, but members of the organizations are strongly encouraged to participate. The mentor and mentee need to develop a partnership. This is prevalent in organizations of today. Mentoring partnerships view both parties freely contributing to the different discussions as equals working together with mutual respect (Shea, 2002). A mentor may still have greater experience, insight and wisdom, but the relationship can be one of sharing. These mentoring relationships are necessary in the fast-paced, ever-changing organizations of today if these organizations are going to be successful.

Research on the impact of mentoring on African American women, from both the perspective of the mentor, as well as the mentee, is needed to increase understanding of the dynamics of the African American woman for personal and professional development.

CHAPTER 2

The Intervention

Mentoring Interventions and Self-Esteem

In this research study, the researcher examined the relationship of mentoring intervention to self-esteem in African American women in light of the daily triple barriers of race, gender and class. This research focus was selected because, although there is research that has studied African Americans, many times, information about African American women has been excluded from the research group. Likewise, studies that research women as a group tend to exclude information that is specific to African American women. This mentoring study focused on African American women being mentored by other African American women. When I researched mentors and the mentoring relationship, the earliest mention of this takes us back to Greek mythology. This example showcases men leading and guiding other men. There may have been examples of women mentoring other women, but it wasn't covered in the history books. If history teaches us anything, women do great things when given the opportunity.

Though Mentor, in Homer's *Odyssey*, was a male guiding and counseling another male, Mentor had a guide: Minerva, or Athena, goddess of wisdom (Duff, 1999). A female took Mentor's form and served as a sidekick and advisor to the young Telemachus. One might wonder how this tale would have played out if Athena had acted as adviser to a young female (Duff, 1999). Female identity and culture distinguish woman-to-woman mentoring relationships from traditional hierarchical man-to-man or man-to-woman mentoring (Duff, 1999). When women can express themselves as women, with women, in the workplace learning connection, women will discover a release of potential that only being genuine can engender (Duff, 1999). Woman-to-woman learning relationships put more emphasis on collaboration rather than hierarchy, more on exchanging gifts than on bestowing wisdom (Duff, 1999).

The scope of the learning for women is broad-based, not limited to career or professional function. Caring, committed woman-to-woman mentoring will consider the wholeness of a woman's life, a life that includes work, family, love, community and spiritual wellbeing (Duff,

1999). The potential for this new form exists with women now looking for a mentor and for women ready and willing to be a mentor (Duff, 1999).

In woman-to-woman mentoring, the connection that takes place often involves the complexities of intimacy that characterize female relationships. Women are drawn to other women because they find someone they like, with whom they can be themselves (Duff, 1999).

The experiences of women of color have been largely neglected as a focus for social science research (Graham, 1992; Reid & Kelly, 1994; Thomas & Miles, 1995). It's time for this information to be shared and communicated. After 17 years of researching this topic, much of this information is still the same. Black women tend to be the only one an organization that are largely dominated by white men. Black women tend to be paid far less than their white women counterparts, regardless of their education and experience.

I have experienced times in my career when my white counterparts were given opportunities to take interim positions when employees would either leave the organization or got promoted. These happened to be positions that I was qualified to do and had also asked to be placed in on an interim basis. During the times they were in these positions, they were given an increase to perform the role, and were kept at that salary, even if they were not successful in keeping the position. The salary was higher for the interim role than my salary for a position I had been doing for many years.

Bond (1997) summed up the following experiences of African American women. She believed the work of women of color should be held together by three primary threads: appreciation for the history as we decipher and interpret the adaptive strategies for women of color; recognition of the intersections of race, gender and class as central to our work; and self-critical examination of the meanings we attach to "differences" (Bond, 1997). Women of color matter and bring such meaning and diversity to the workplace that, when they are not part of the workplace, there is a huge void.

Women of color come together as a group to acknowledge and protect the 'inner me,' the self-voice inside that tells them "what they need to be about" (Duff, 1999). Black women often talk about being spiritual. Spirituality does not necessarily mean religiosity; it simply means that there is a belief that there are beings that are greater than them. African Americans as a group understand that concept of spirituality and it is a means of support (Duff, 1999). These women come together to encourage and learn from one another in a way that is consistent with their history. When Black women come together as a group, they can feel comfortable being themselves (Duff, 1999). African American women have been separated from their history. Duff (1999) stated, "In the African American tradition, each one would teach what she knows. Elder women were the mentors. They gave what they knew. Their degrees came from living, not from schooling". Learning and growing often means taking some action. Learning, growing and taking action will give them a better tomorrow (Duff, 1999).

More often than not, African American women who have been mentored have had White males serving in the mentor role. The number of women and minorities, who have been mentors in high-level corporate positions, is limited (Ibarra, 1993; Duff, 1999). Thomas (1990), in his study of race and mentoring relationships, found African Americans in upper-level positions comprised less than 5% of the total number of professionals in the stratum and that White men predominately served as mentors to all four race-gender groups he studied: White men, African American men, African American women and White women.

Self-Esteem

Self-esteem seems to be connected to two broad dimensions of human behavior: positive and negative mental health (Murk, 1999). This vital human phenomenon is often understood in relation to positive mental health and general psychological well-being. Research in this area correlates high self-esteem with such things as: positive ego functioning, good personal adjustment and internal sense of control, the likelihood of a favorable outcome for psychotherapy, healthy adjustment to aging, individual autonomy, and a tendency toward androgyny (Bednar, Wells, & Peterson, 1989; Coopersmith, 1967; Mruk, 1999). An example of high self-esteem is when one has a great sense of themselves and a positive outlook on their lives. Another example of high self-esteem can also be that one is in touch with their inner person, their overall well-being, and has an incredibly good outlook on their life. The lack of self-esteem is often related to a number of important negative possibilities, such as: feelings of inadequacy, a sense of unworthiness, increased anxiety, depression, suicide, child abuse of all types, exploitative relationships among adults, and certain mental health disorders (Coopersmith, 1967; Skager & Kerst, 1989; Mruk, 1999). When one is experiencing a lack of self-esteem, they are displaying behavior that makes one feel less than. One's outlook of themselves is extremely negative to the point that the person may seem like someone else.

Satir (1988) believed self-esteem is a concept, an attitude, a feeling, an image; and it is represented by behavior. Self-esteem is the ability to value one's self and to treat one's self with dignity, love and reality. Integrity, honesty, responsibility, compassion, love and competence all flow easily from people who have high self-esteem. When an individual feels that she or he matters, there is the feeling that the world is a better place because she or he is in it (Satir, 1988). When self-worth is appreciated, individuals are ready to see and respect the worth of others. It is important to remember that even people with high self-esteem have moments when they can feel low. The difference is that people who on occasion feel low do not generally view themselves as worthless, and they do not deny that these low feelings exist (Satir, 1988; Crocker, 1998).

Knowing that change is possible, and committing oneself to change, is an important concept. There is always hope that one's life can change because there are always new things to learn (Satir, 1988). Satir (1988) put these feelings and ideas about self-worth in a declaration entitled, *I Am Me* (see end of book).

Mentoring Interventions

Role modeling is perceived as a positive mentoring intervention. The importance of role models for women's development is evident in a variety of areas, including achievement in mathematics and science (Boli, Allen & Payne, 1985; Gibson and Cordova, 1999), healthy identity formation (Komarovsky, 1985), pursuit of nontraditional fields of study, such as science and mathematics (Maples, 1992), as well as leadership (Astin & Leland, 1991; Keohane, 1984; Bowman, et al., 1999). Shandley (1989) recounted the history of the term mentor: The term mentor has its root in Homer's Greek epic poem, "The Odyssey". In this myth, Odysseus, a great royal warrior, had been off fighting the Trojan War and entrusted the care of his son Telemachus to his friend and advisor, Mentor. Mentor was charged with advising and serving as a guardian to the entire royal household. As the story unfolds, Mentor accompanies and guides Telemachus on a journey in search of his father and, ultimately, of a new and fuller identity of his own. Since this time, the word mentor has become synonymous with wise teacher, guide, philosopher and friend. (Huang & Lynch, 1995; Duff, 1999).

Throughout history, there is documentation of individuals who have been influenced by mentors. For centuries, the predominant population to be mentored has been men. In the United States, they have been Anglo men. During the mid to late 1970s, mentoring has become more common for women and minorities. Mentoring has been primarily centered on career development in the business world. Mentoring has become an extremely popular intervention with youth and, in particular, disadvantaged youth. Philips and Hendry (1996) believed that studies support that mentoring can be helpful to young people in general as they make the transition into adulthood. Mentors have effectively been used to affect the academic success of students (Jacobi, 1991; Bowman, et al., 1999). Mentors have been used in leadership development, as well (Shandley, 1989; Murrell, et al., 1999).

Although no studies could be found using mentoring as an intervention for self-esteem development, there are four issues and concerns. First, the concern is that there is no definitive definition of mentoring. Jacobi (1991) noted that from three disciplines—business, education, and psychology—there were fifteen different definitions.

Second, the concern is that there is no specific age specified for the mentor (Murrell, et al., 1999). In some studies, the mentor is a peer; in others, the mentor is seven to ten years older than the mentee.

Third, the concern is that no criterion documents what the duration period for the mentoring intervention should be. In some cases, a mentor and mentee only met on one occasion. Other mentors/mentees had met more frequently, and their relationships lasted, in some cases, up to ten years.

Finally, the concern is on how intense and how intimate a mentoring relationship should be. The literature is divided on the significance of the similarity of gender and ethnicity in the mentoring relationship. Jacobi (1991) cites one final difference, which is the value of self-selection and free choice versus a mentor that was assigned (Duff, 1999; Murrell, et al., 1999).

There are several insights to be gained from the literature, as well. Mentoring encompasses a total of twelve functions or skills. These twelve functions are: brokering relationships, building relationships and maintaining relationships, coaching, communicating, encouraging, facilitating, goal setting, guiding, managing conflict, problem-solving, providing and receiving feedback, and reflecting (Zachary, 2001). Not all mentoring experiences contain all twelve elements, but generally fall into one of the three areas: emotional and psychological support, direct assistance with career and professional development, and role modeling (Duff, 1999).

The research indicated that mentoring has four benefits: a helpful relationship that usually focuses on achievement; mentoring is a reciprocal relationship, with each individual gaining some benefit; mentoring is personal; and mentors show greater experience, influence and achievement with a particular organization or environment (Jacobi, 1991; Duff, 1999).

The research indicated that although minority women and men showed they could benefit most from the mentoring experience, many times, it can be exceedingly difficult in finding the correct or appropriate matches as it relates to gender and ethnicity. Women and minorities tend to choose Anglo men as mentors, relying on the notion that they have a better understanding of the system, are well respected, and have a better chance of getting ahead faster all because of their mentorship by an Anglo man (Jacobi, 1991; Duff, 1999). Mentoring was not equally available to women in the workplace (Blake, 1998; Duff, 1999).

Through the use of mentoring intervention programs, the following benefits resulted: mentors set high expectations of performance, offer challenging ideas, help build self-confidence, encourage professional behavior, offer friendship, confront negative behaviors and attitudes, listen to personal problems, teach by example, provide growth experiences, offer quotable quotes, explain how the organization works, coach their mentees, stand by their mentees in critical situations, offer wise counsel, encourage winning behaviors, trigger self-awareness, inspire their mentees, share critical knowledge, offer encouragement, and assist with mentees' careers (Shea, 1997; Blake,1998; Duff, 1999).

Black Women and Mentoring

Mentoring is defined by Thomas (1990) as the relationship between juniors and seniors (in terms of age or experience) that exists primarily to support the personal (or psychosocial) and career development of the junior person. Mentoring relationships provide a wide range of developmental functions (including coaching and counseling) and require both individuals to invest considerable time and emotion in the relationship (Blake, 1998).

Mentoring has become extremely popular in organizational settings. The past ten years have seen a proliferation of research investigating the effects of mentoring on a variety of organizational outcomes (Burke, 1984; Burke & McKeen, 1989; Dresser & Ash, 1990; Dunbar, 1990; Hill & Kamprath, 1991; Kram, 1985; Kram & Hall, 1989; Kram & Isabella, 1985; Missrian, 1982; Noe, 1988; Thomas, 1989; Zey, 1984; Blake, 1998). Much of the early work in mentoring research has been done using White male samples (Collins & Scott, 1978; Dalton, Thomas & Price, 1977; Gould, 1972; Levinson, et al., 1978; Roche, 1979; Blake, 1998).

Many scholars have realized that women who would like to have a mentoring relationship tend to be faced with many obstacles and challenges. This is most commonly due to gender biases. Literature has been developed to address the concerns of women in the mentoring process (Clawson & Kram, 1984; Collins, 1983; Fitt & Newton, 1981; Halcomb, 1980; Nieva & Gutek, 1981; Noe, 1986; Ragins, 1989; Duff, 1999). Most of the studies covered in this literature have included White women. Many scholars have researched mentoring experiences for African American managers in the corporate sector (Cox & Nkomo, 1991; Davis & Watson, 1982; Deinard & Friedman, 1991; Hill & Kampath, 1991; Ibarra, 1993; Thomas, 1989, 1990; Blake, 1998). Yet, the voices of African American women, which are different from those of African Americans who happen to be men, and different from those of women who happen to be White, are still largely unheard (Blake, 1998).

Blake (1998) conducted an analysis of the mentoring experiences of African American professional women in the corporate setting. Through informal interviews, a number of themes emerged concerning African American women's experiences of mentoring (Blake, 1998). Two prominent themes were the following: (a) there was a general lack of African American role models who might serve as mentors for women involved in the study; and (b) African American women's relationships with White women mentors are largely characterized by mistrust, which may be grounded on the historical interaction between women of these cultural groups (Blake, 1998). Professional African American women are often pioneering, jumping into new territories, as they move into middle and upper management. Most times, this is done without any assistance from African American women who have preceded them. The guidance, support and information regarding informal practices that mentoring offered these women was critical (Blake, 1998).

Black Women and Self-Esteem

Self-esteem is an important indicator of one's self-image. It has important implications for psychological well-being, as well as educational and professional aspirations (Carter, 2001). Echoing the familiar African proverb, "It takes a village to raise a child", there is a philosophy that says, "It takes a village to sustain a black woman" (Green, 2001). Several attempts have been made to better understand the contributing factors to the development of African American women's self-esteem.

Gainor and Forrest (1991); Henriques & Calhoun (1999) used a multiple self-reliant model to explain the formation of self-concept in African American women's self-esteem. Threats or support to self-esteem, such as parenting, the mother-daughter relationship, male-female relationships, and racial identity were explored. Harris (1995), Henriques & Calhoun (1999) addressed self, family and socio-cultural factors that influence positive or negative body-image attitudes of African American women. Harris (1992) explored a model of development for African American females that has three key elements, remarkably similar to the overall strategies found used by African American and Caucasian women to build and maintain self-esteem (Chatham-Carpenter & DeFrancisco, 1997; Henriques & Calhoun, 1999). These elements included: (a) sense of self-identity developed through both individual and collective accomplishments; (b) sense of control, especially as it relates to dealing with racism; and (c) sense of belonging or interdependence.

Community support seems to act as an important ingredient in the development of self-esteem in many African American women. The traditional Black church has served as a primary source of positive identity and social support (Peterson, 1992; Allen, 2001). Many times, the African American family is seen as a system functioning in crisis. But this unit is also a support system. The value of community is highly imbedded and common in the African American culture and heritage, where groupness, cooperation and collective responsibility are emphasized (Asante, 1988; Boykins, Jagers, Ellison, & Albury, 1997; Greene, 1994; Jackson et al., 1997; Jagers & Mock, 1995; Kim, Triandis, Kagitcibasi, Choi, & Yoon, 1994; Nobles, 1980; Allen, 2001).

Mentoring Intervention Programs and Leaders

To have a successful intervention program, the facilitator needs to have a good understanding of leadership and how to be a good leader. Warren Bennis (1988) wrote, "Leaders learn by leading, and they learn best in the face of obstacles. As weather shapes mountains, problems shape leaders. Difficult bosses, lack of vision and virtue in the executive suite, circumstances beyond their control, and their own mistakes have been the leaders' basic curriculum".

In the 21st century, leaders will face many issues. Leaders must be equipped to handle the changes that emerge. A leader will need certain traits and attributes to succeed. Kouzes and Posner (2002) asked the following open-ended question: "What values (personal traits or characteristics) do you look for and admire in your leader?" Of twenty responses received, the top four characteristics of a leader were: to be honest, forward-thinking, competent and inspiring (Kouzes & Posner, 2002). These four characteristics were identified by 50% of the respondents.

Other characteristics and traits identified in the survey were: to be intelligent, fair-minded, broadminded, supportive, straightforward, dependable, cooperative, determined, imaginative, ambitious, courageous, caring, mature, loyal, self-controlled and independent (Kouzes & Posner, 2002). Kouzes & Posner (2002) spoke of the Five Practices of Exemplary Leadership. These five practices are to: (a) model the way, (b) inspire a vision, (c) challenge the process, (d) enable others to act, and (e) encourage the heart. Leaders model the way by effectively modeling the behavior they expect of others. Leaders must first be clear about their guiding principles (Kouzes & Posner, 2002).

Leaders inspire a shared vision. To enlist people into a vision, leaders must know their constituents and speak their language. Leaders challenge the process. The leader's primary contribution is the recognition of good ideas, support of those ideas, and the willingness to challenge the system to get new products, processes, services and systems adopted (Kouzes & Posner, 2002).

Exemplary leaders enable others to act. They foster collaboration and build trust. This sense of teamwork goes far beyond a few direct reports or close confidants. They engage those who make the project work—and in some way, who must live with the results. Leaders encourage the hearts of their constituents to carry on. Genuine acts of caring uplift the spirit and draw people forward. It is part of the leader's job to show appreciation for the people's contribution and to create a culture of celebration (Kouzes & Posner, 2002). As leaders emerge in the 21st century, they must take a look at the vision and value throughout the organization. Leaders must be consistent with their co-leaders and speak in one voice. Leaders need to have shared values for the organization for both the personal and organizational side of the business.

Exercising shared values in an organization has many advantages to the leader. Some such advantages are: fostering strong feelings of personal effectiveness, promoting high levels of loyalty in an organization, facilitating consensus about key organizational goals and the organizational stakeholders, encouraging ethical behavior, promoting strong norms about working hard and caring, reducing levels of job stress and tension, fostering pride in an organization, facilitating understanding about job expectations, fostering teamwork and esprit de corps (Hesselbein, 1996; Kouzes & Posner, 2002).

Leaders will need to adapt to the changing roles and relationships in society to be successful in their jobs. Effective leaders in years to come will have strong values and beliefs that will be shared with individuals as they grow. Leaders will be visionaries and will believe strongly that they can and should be shaping the future. They will act on their beliefs through their personal behavior (Hesselbein, 1996; Kouzes & Posner, 2001). Leaders should be diverse to address the changes in culture and better understand the people available to them in the work community. Leaders should be trained across cultures and view differences as strengths to grow on, not weaknesses (Kouzes & Posner, 2002).

Leaders of the future can win the war on the emerging changes being thrown at them. Leaders must be persistent and pay attention to the ever-changing world they live in. Leaders must never stop learning. Keeping all of these things in mind will give the leaders of tomorrow a fighting chance.

Black Women and Leadership

Leadership development for women is often intended to help break through the so-called "glass ceiling" of invisible, but formidable workplace barriers (Shaw, Champlin, Hartmann & Spalter-Roth, 1993; Green, 2001). For women of African descent in the United States, however, the metaphorical ceiling blocking their career advancement may be more than mere glass—indeed some have likened it more to concrete (Anderson, 1998). African American women need programs of leadership that will aid them in penetrating and breaking through workplace barriers ranging from subtle racist attitudes and prejudices to blatant discriminatory practices (Green, 2001). These programs can seek to create a unique, caring, positive and self-affirming "village" in which African American women can take collective responsibility for, and assume leadership in, identifying and challenging barriers to their career advancement (Green, 2001). African American women need to mentor, and be mentored by, their "sister colleagues" and assume responsibility for affirming each other's efforts to survive and thrive in the workplace (Greene, 2001).

Wood (1997) contended that women need experience with, and exposure to, female leadership models to encourage them to aspire to leadership positions. Bell and

Nkomo (1999) argued that women acquire experience with female role models through access to formal and informal decision-making structures in the workplace. Use of both of these strategies will empower African American women. African American women need numerous opportunities to become familiar with women in leadership roles who are involved in formal and informal decision-making activities throughout the workplace (Green, 2001).

Career advancement and leadership development for African American women should be based on the empowerment model. The empowerment model helps one understand how they can use what they already possess to move themselves closer to where they wish to be in their lives. According to Fong & Furuto (2001), empowerment involves helping people "to discover and use the resources within and around them, and to seize some control over their lives and the decisions that are critical to their lives". They further asserted that, to be empowered, a woman needs a nurturing environment that gives her viable options to make choices about her career (Fung and Furuto, 2001). Empowered women, Collins (2000) maintained, assume authority to select from among those options and, as Gutierrez (1990) noted, the more options women have for developing their skills and abilities, the greater their sense of empowerment.

To this end, Green (2001) believed that African American women mentors and mentees need to work toward developing a more positive and potent sense of self and personal power by showing them how to take risks, link personal and political power, recognize and build on existing strengths, and create a support network; attain the knowledge and skills needed for a more critical comprehension of the social, political and economic realities and constraints of the workplace environment; and, make use of resources and specific strategies to attain personal career goals and the collective goal of improving the workplace of others.

This research let us know that none of us makes it through this life alone. We need each other to learn and grow. We need each other to gain a better sense of who we are as individuals. As you work and learn from others, you find yourself. You learn what is important for your own personal success and growth. You also learn that one size doesn't fit all, but you will be able to understand what works for you. You can better understand and define your uniqueness as you enhance who you are. You can use the tools you have learned to excel and become your best self.

CHAPTER 3

Methods of Mentorship & Self-Esteem

T he research design study focused on the mentor relationship intervention and self-esteem (Creswell, 2002). This research study analyzed data of the control group of twenty non-mentees and an experimental group of twenty mentees (forty participants in total). This model was chosen to show that if there is focus and attention given to working on building self-esteem through working with a mentor and the mentoring process, you can indeed improve the level of one's self esteem. Also, by having a group that didn't receive mentoring, it shows that if there is not attention given to building self-esteem, there will be little or no change.

African American women have limited opportunities to interact with other African American women in the workplace due to the lack of Black women in managerial positions (Cuff, 1999). As a result, Black women often lack mentoring relationships with members of their race and

as it provides important information on the degree to which a person is defensively inflating his or her self-presentation (O'Brien & Epstein, 1988).

The defensive self-enhancement scale differentiates between an incredibly high and defensively high self-esteem. The MSEI is an objective self-report inventory, which provides measures of the components of self-esteem (Epstein, 1980). MSEI was used as a pretest and asked mentees to answer the question of what self-esteem meant to them. The instrument was selected because it helps to give an understanding of self-esteem and what causes or affects self-esteem to increase or decrease in someone. It shows that there are many dimensions that affect the levels of self-esteem. By gaining an understanding of these different areas, you can get a better grasp on how self-esteem affects you.

Methodology Appropriateness

Black women volunteered for the program. This study took place in Pontiac, Michigan at a local Black church named The Deliverance Church of God in Christ. The Black women who mentored where college-educated or were highly respected in the church. The mentors worked in a variety of industries, such as higher education, corporate America, non-profits, healthcare, teaching and music ministry. Many of the women in this study attended services at this local church or had visited this church on several occasions.

The volunteer recruitment included flyers distributed at local businesses, word-of-mouth from recruits, and recruits from community-based programs using flyers posted in a community center.

Mentors were selected based on criteria discussed in Faddis' (1998) *Hand and Hand: Mentoring Women*. Some characteristics of the mentor included: self-awareness and self-confidence with regard to both work and interaction with others; high standards and expectations of oneself and one's colleagues; enthusiasm and a sense of humor; and clear and effective communication skills, including the ability to express a point, defend a position and confront hard issues, without becoming overly aggressive or judgmental. Above all, mentors had to believe in the potential of the young, inexperienced or the disadvantaged to make positive contributions.

The twenty participants in the experimental group engaged in the five components of the intervention model, including the: (a) focusing phase, (b) awareness phase, (c) enhancing phase, (d) enhancing phase-II, and (e) management phase. The intervention program consisted of the following five themes for five weeks: (a) becoming aware of self-esteem, (b) appreciating self-esteem, (c) increasing worthiness, (d) increasing competence, and (e) maintaining self-esteem (Mruk, 1999). Topics related to the workshop themes were discussed based on the conversation and questions that were generated out of the discussion phases of this intervention. Some examples of the topics discussed included body image, ideal weight, sterotypes of Black women, dating, challenges of being a single mothers, and racism, to name a few.

Forty women were recruited to participate in this research study. Recruitment was done through word of mouth and announcements at local community events, churches and businesses. The sample population was determined based on the Participant Response Form. A group of forty individuals gathered at a local community-based organization. The participants signed the research consent and expectation forms. Groups were divided into a control group and an experimental group based on random assignment.

Mentors

Twenty participants were paired with mentors. Mentors in this study agreed to participate because they wanted to be a part of the research study that showcases Black women. This is the first study that focuses on Black women mentoring Black women. When I discussed the significance of this project, and the premise that took a deeper look at the connection between self-esteem and mentoring among Black women, these mentors were intrigued to participate.

Mentors and Mentees

Each mentee/mentor pair received an orientation to the mentor/mentee process. They each signed a contract outlining minimal expectations of the mentor/mentee relationship. Each mentee was issued a journal in which to log contact with the mentor. They were instructed to assess journal writing after each theme was presented. Each theme was assigned on a scale of one to five. Contact with the mentors was made by telephone, mail note, e-mail, or in person. The mentees were asked to write a brief summary of the contact, noting: (a) the length of time of the contact; (b) feelings about the interaction; and (c) any other pertinent comments that were appropriate concerning the contact.

Experimental Group

After five weeks of contact, the journals were collected, and a posttest of the MSEI was administered, along with answering the question of what self-esteem meant to them. The pre- and posttest were scored and analyzed according to the nine attributes of the MSEI: (a) competence, (b) lovability, (c) likeability, (d) personal power, (e) self-control, (f) moral self-approval, (g) body appearance, and (h) body function. In addition to the MSEI, the researcher interviewed the mentees to gain a better understanding of their perspective of the mentoring intervention experience.

Control Group

At the conclusion of five weeks, the control group was administered the MSEI. This group received no intervention. The pre- and posttests were scored and analyzed according to the nine attributes of the MSEI. The interview questions and journals were only relevant to the intervention methodology; therefore, the control group was not interviewed, nor did they keep a journal.

Feasibility and Appropriateness

The tests were administered at the beginning of the program and on the last day of the program. The tests took approximately one half-hour. The groups consisted of twenty individuals for the control group, as well as for the experimental group. There were twenty mentors for the experimental group. There was a total of forty participants. Workshop materials were used to compare and contrast the intervention group and the non-intervention group. The MSEI was used to compare and contrast the two groups. The pretest and posttest data were used, as well as other personal data, such as age, background, highest level of education completed, family information, and more that was collected from both of the groups. Session drawings for prizes were held for on-time arrivers to ensure consistent class attendance.

The goal of this study was to show that one's self-esteem could be built through mentoring and that there was a positive relationship between self-esteem and mentoring. Now, we'll talk about the findings of the intervention.

CHAPTER 4

Presentation and Research Analysis

entoring is defined by Thomas (1990) as the relationship between juniors and seniors (in terms of age or experience) that exists primarily to support the personal (or psychosocial) and career development of the junior person. Self-esteem is defined as the ability to value one's self and to treat one's self with dignity, love and reality.

There were five components of the mentoring intervention model—the focusing phase, awareness phase, enhancing phase, enhancing phase II, and management phase. The intervention program focused on five themes over five weeks: becoming aware of self-esteem, appreciating self-esteem, increasing worthiness, increasing competence, and maintaining self-esteem (Mruk,1999). Topics that emerged during the workshops, related to the workshop themes, were discussed based on the conversations and questions that were generated out of the discussion phases of the mentoring workshops.

Self-esteem was defined by Mruk's (1999) typology of definitions, which consists of four ways of defining self-esteem: attitudinal approach, the different sets of attitudes, psychological responses, and function or components of personality.

Attitudinal approach means treating the self as an object of attention, for we have positive and negative cognitive, emotional and behavioral reactions to ourselves just as we do to other objects in the world (Mruk, 1999). An example of this might be how one might feel about their looks or their body size or shape.

The different sets of attitudes are the discrepancy of what one wishes to be—the "ideal" self—and what one currently sees, the "real" or "perceived" self (Mruk, 1999). This might be represented by someone who wears a small size but perceives themselves as a larger size based on how they see themselves.

Psychological responses are usually described as feeling-based or affective in nature, such as positive versus negative or accepting versus rejecting (Mruk, 1999). This deals with how one is affected when something positive or negative is said to them or about them. Examples of these responses are anger, moodiness, irritability, becoming obsessive, crying, denial, disbelief, disinterest in previous activities, emotional numbness and forgetfulness.

A function, or a component, of personality is where self-esteem is seen as a part of the self-system, usually one that is concerned with motivation and/or self-regulation (Mruk, 1999). This involves controlling one's behavior, emotions and thoughts in pursuit of long-term goals. Self-regulation also refers to the ability to manage disruptive emotions and impulses. An example of this might be one have difficulty getting up early to work out, but you do so as a way of improving fitness.

By using the MSEI as pre- and posttests, it was possible to determine the women's feelings regarding five themes: becoming aware of self-esteem, appreciating self-esteem, increasing worthiness, increasing competence, and maintaining self-esteem based on their mentoring experience (Mruk, 1999). The MSEI was developed to provide a multidimensional measure of self-esteem. The MSEI measures eleven domains: global self-esteem (GSE), competence (CMP), lovability (LVE), likeability (LKE), self-control (SFC), personal power (PWR), moral self-approval (MOR), body appearance (BAP), body functioning (BFN), (identity integration (IDN), and defensive self-enhancement (DEF).

The global self-esteem scale directly measures the subject's overall feelings about herself by asking about generalized feelings of positive self-worth and inadequacy (O'Brien & Epstein, 1988). Competence is defined as "competent; feels capable of mastering new tasks; learns quickly and does well at most things, feels talented, feels effective and capable" (O'Brien & Epstein, 1988. Lovability is defined as "worthy of love; feels cared for by loved ones; accepted as a person and counts on support from loved ones; able to express and receive feelings of love; involved in a satisfying intimate relationship" (O'Brien & Epstein, 1988). Likeability is defined as "likable, popular, accepted by peers and included in their plans; enjoyable; companion; gets along well with others; popular in dating situations; expects to be liked; makes a good first impression" (O'Brien & Epstein, 1988).

Self-control is defined as "self-discipline; preserving; good at setting and achieving goals; not easily distracted; in control of emotions; exercises restraint in eating, drinking and/or the use of drugs" (O'Brien & Epstein, 1988, p. 6). Personal power is defined as "powerful; successfully seeks positions of leadership; good at influencing others' opinions and behaviors; assertive; has strong impact on others" (O'Brien & Epstein, 1988). Body functioning is defined as "well-coordinated; agile; in good physical condition;

comfortable with body; enjoys physical activities, such as dancing or sports; feeling healthy and feels a sense of vitality and vigor in body functioning" (O'Brien & Epstein, 1988). Identity integrations focus is on the overall functioning, or adequacy, of the self-concept (O'Brien & Epstein, 1988).

Table 1

Outline of Domains and Themes by Week of Intervention

MSEI DOMAIN	THEME	WEEK
Global self-esteem (GSE)	Overall Self-Esteem	Week 1
Competence (CMP)	Becoming Aware of Self-Esteem	Week 1
Lovability (LVE)	Appreciating Self-Esteem	Week 2
Likeability (LKE)	Increasing Self-worthiness	Week 3
Self-control (SFC)	Increasing Self-worthiness	Week 3
Personal power (PWR)	Increasing Competence	Week 4
Moral self-approval (MOR)	Increasing Competence	Week 4
Body appearance (BAP)	Maintaining Self-Esteem	Week 5
Body functioning (BFN)	Maintaining Self-Esteem	Week 5
Identity integration (IDN)	Maintaining Self-Esteem	Week 5
Defensive self-enhancement (DEF)	Maintaining Self-Esteem	Week 5

Table 1 identifies each of the eleven domains of the MSEI as they related to the five themes of the research study. The five themes were introduced each week in the five-week intervention program.

Data from surveys, observations and questionnaires were collected to determine whether or not there was a relationship between a mentoring intervention program and the self-esteem of Black women.

Research Questions

Five research questions guided this study. The questions are as follows:

1. To what degree will mentoring intervention affect the self-esteem (MSEI) of African American women?

2. To what degree will becoming aware of self-esteem affect the self-esteem (MSEI) of African American women?

3. To what degree will appreciating self-esteem affect the self-esteem (MSEI) of African American women?

4. To what degree will increasing worthiness affect the self-esteem (MSEI) of African American women?

5. To what degree will maintaining self-esteem affect the self-esteem (MSEI) of African American women?

Mentors and Mentees

The mentor/mentee relationship gave the mentors and the mentees the opportunity to pair up with the mentors to build a mentoring relationship. The mentors and mentees were randomly paired so that the study could be totally objective. Journals were used to record the mentoring experience, and the mentors and mentees agreed on a contact schedule over the five-week period that worked for both parties involved. Each mentee/mentor pair received an orientation of the process. They each signed a contract, outlining minimal expectations of the mentor/mentee relationship. It was exciting to see the group read through the material and get a better understanding of the process. The mentors and mentees took time to talk briefly and exchange contact information with each other.

Each mentee was issued a writing journal to log contact with the mentor. They were instructed to write an assessment on each of the five workshops. The workshops were held weekly, and each covered a specific theme. Using a Likert scale, the workshops were assessed on a scale of one to five—one classified as "not good or needs additional work" and five indicating "excellent or very good".

Training

An informational meeting was held for the mentees and their mentors. At the meeting for the mentees, specific responsibilities were discussed, such as group guidelines and expectations. Group guidelines and expectations included respect, attendance and participation. Mentees were instructed to make the initial contact with the mentor.

After each contact, mentees recorded reflections, thoughts and ideas in their journals about the topic they discussed with their mentors. Mentors and mentees were instructed to meet a minimum of two hours each week for five weeks.

The training meeting included a discussion of additional expectations, including progress reports from the mentees at the designated times that would be decided upon between the mentor and the mentee during the five weeks; and participation in an interview about the experience, if they desired. Each of the mentees and mentors had the opportunity to be interviewed if they were willing to share information outside the group interaction. The interview process was optional, but many agreed to take part in the process.

In speaking with the mentors, I found that they had all performed some sort of mentoring in the past.

This meeting was used to build the foundation for a focused, supportive environment. It was important that the mentees felt comfortable sharing information about themselves among the group. The mentoring intervention was structured to facilitate interest and build a comfort zone among the mentees. The intervention was also structured, by the workshops, to raise consciousness of individual self-esteem and the role that self-esteem plays in lives. The first task in any good, systematic self-esteem enhancement program is to raise the consciousness of individual self-esteem (Mruk, 1999).

The program model provided African American women with mentoring support and ways of increasing their levels of self-esteem, as well as maintaining their self-esteem. The self-esteem intervention program included workshops, assessments and candid discussions from African American professional women to assist in ensuring the successful completion of the program. The mentors were experienced professionals. Some of the mentors came from a psychology/clinical background and felt comfortable mentoring and counseling the mentees. Some of the mentors were experienced teachers with credentials. Other mentors had experience in family therapy and support.

Data Collection

Three sources of data were collected during this research study: Multidimensional Self-Esteem Inventory (MSEI), journals completed by experimental participants (mentees), and data collected from the intervention group subject interviews (mentors and mentees). The questions and journal entries were based solely on the intervention, so the control group was not asked the questions or asked to keep a journal.

The MSEI tests were administered at the beginning of the program and on the last day of the program. They were administered in the classroom setting in the community center. The test took approximately one half-hour.

The test (pre and post) from the MSEI was collected on two separate occasions from each of the participants in the study. The first collection of the data, the pretest, was during the first week of the intervention. The second collection of data served as a posttest during week five of the intervention. Data from the mentors and the mentees was collected throughout the five weeks of the intervention. Both the experimental group and the control group began with twenty participants (mentees) and twenty mentors. After the study, sixteen participants in the experimental group and nineteen in the control group remained. The results of the data analysis are presented in order of the research questions. Therefore, only thirty-five participants were included in the analysis. As a result of scheduling conflicts and other obligations, four mentees from the experimental group and one participant from the control group decided not to continue the study.

Intervention

The intervention consisted of a five-week-long relationship between the mentor and the mentee (experimental group). The mentoring relationship included the following:

1. Ongoing contact with mentor and mentee. Contact would be established by the mentee.

2. Journal records of reflections, thoughts and ideas by the mentees regarding the topic discussions with their mentors.

3. Minimum of four hours of contact over five weeks.

Experimental Group

At the conclusion of five weeks of contact, the journal assessments of the five workshop themes, the posttest of the MSEI and the open-ended question of what self-esteem means were collected. The pretest and posttest were scored and analyzed according to the nine attributes of the MSEI— competence, lovability, likeability, personal power, self-control, moral self-approval, body appearance and body function. In addition to the MSEI, the researcher interviewed the mentee to gain a better understanding of their perspective of the mentoring intervention experience.

Control Group

Concluding five weeks, the control group was administered the MSEI. This group received no intervention. The pre and posttest was scored and analyzed according to the nine attributes of the MSEI.

Processing and Analysis of the Research Data

An independent comparison was used to analyze the difference in mean scores, between the experimental group and the control group, on the posttests.

The data in this chapter is presented in the order of the research questions. The five questions were answered by using a combination of comments from the journals and interviews, and the MSEI results. The journals and interview data were also used as supportive data based on the participant's beliefs and perceptions gathered during the mentoring intervention.

Analysis by Research Questions

The following research questions guided this study.

1. To what degree will mentoring intervention affect the self-esteem (MSEI) of African American women?

2. To what degree will becoming aware of self-esteem affect the self-esteem (MSEI) of African American women?

3. To what degree will appreciating self-esteem affect the self-esteem (MSEI) of African American women?

4. To what degree will increasing worthiness affect the self-esteem (MSEI) of African American women?

5. To what degree will maintaining self-esteem affect the self-esteem (MSEI) of African American women?

The research questions were analyzed using the eleven domains of the MSEI.

1. **To what degree will mentoring intervention affect the self-esteem (MSEI) of African American women?**

This question was answered using the global self-esteem (GSE) scale of the MSEI. This scale directly measures the subject's overall feelings about herself by asking about generalized feelings of positive self-worth and inadequacy (O'Brien & Epstein, 1988). The global self-esteem data was also aligned with the journal writing of the mentees. The difference between the sample mean scores of both groups (experimental and control), for the posttests was analyzed by a one tail T-score. Only criteria GSE showed significance.

There were significant differences between the posttests of the participants in the experimental group for global self-esteem and the control group. Journal writing from the experimental group support this data. The journal writing indicated that the mentoring intervention was "beneficial and worth the experience." One participant wrote, "This mentoring intervention, as well as working with my mentor, helped me to realize some things I already knew to be true for me, but this experience added more support to this belief."

2. To what degree will becoming aware of self-esteem affect the self-esteem (MSEI) of African American women?

The mentees, through the mentoring intervention, became aware of their self-esteem and, as a result, showed significant increases in their self-esteem. Learning what positively affected their self-esteem helped the mentees to work on those things to continue to build on increasing their self-esteem.

3. To what degree will appreciating self-esteem affect the self-esteem (MSEI) of African American women?

The characteristics of competence (CMP) is defined as "competent; feels capable of mastering new tasks; learns quickly and does well at most things; feels talented; feels effective and capable" (O'Brien & Epstein, 1988).

There were significant differences between the pre- and posttests for participants in the experimental for the competence (CMP) characteristic. The competence scale also addresses research Question 3; the significance in difference determined an improvement of competence of 6.01%.

The journal entries, written by the mentees, supported this result and included: "I'm not sure that I will continue my education to the master or doctorate level. But I know if I choose to go that far, I can aspire to do anything. It's all about what you want out of life."

There was no statistical significance that occurred within the control group between the pre- and posttest. This analysis supports the expectation that there would be no statistically significant differences because the control group did not receive the mentoring intervention. At less than 5%, the difference between the control group pre- and posttest was not significant.

There was a difference that occurred within the experimental group between the pre and posttests. The likeability analysis supports research question three. The difference was slight and showed an improvement of 0.16%. Although there was only a slight difference in this area, through the journal entries and the interview questions, it was determined that the mentees' feelings indicated, "They were secure in their relationships and felt very comfortable." Another mentee added, "If they wanted to hang out with their guy and his friends, they did. If they wanted to just be with the girls, they felt comfortable to do this, as well. No pressure either way." One mentee explained, "The comfort level comes in a relationship when you're with the right person who fits your style."

No differences occurred within the control group between the pre- and posttests. This supports the expectation that the control group would not show any statistical significance because they were not mentored in the mentoring intervention. The characteristic identity integration (IDN) is defined as a "clear sense of identity; knows who she is; knows what she wants out of life; well-defined long-term goals; inner sense of cohesion and integration of different aspects of self-concept" (O'Brien & Epstein, 1988).

A well-functioning self-concept is associated with a tendency to seek out and assimilate new experiences, thereby allowing the self-concept to continually grow and expand. The identity integration scale measures an individual's view of her efficiency in assimilating new information and in organizing and directing life experience. The scale is similar to the global self-esteem scale in that its focus is on the overall functioning, or adequacy, of the self-concept (O'Brien & Epstein, 1988).

There was a significant difference between the pre- and posttests of the experimental group for the identity integration (IDN) characteristic. Many, if not all, of the mentees had a clear understanding of who they were and what life holds for them. One mentee mentioned, "Carpe'

Diem" which means seizing the moment and living life to the fullest. Another mentee mentioned that she always wanted to be in a position to get the most out of life and what it has to offer. The identity integration (IDN) characteristic showed improvement at 2.21%.

No statistically significant difference occurred within the control group between the pre- and posttests. This supports the expectation that the control group would show no statistically significant difference because they were not mentored in the mentoring intervention.

4. **To what degree will increasing worthiness affect the self-esteem (MSEI) of African American women?**

Research Question 4 is answered using the characteristics of: (a) lovability (LVE), (b) likeability (LKE), (c) body appearance (BAP), (d) body functioning (BFN), and (e) personal power (PWR).

The characteristic of lovability is defined as "worthy of love; feels cared for by loved ones; accepted as a person; and counts on support from loved ones; able to express and receive feelings of love; involved in a satisfying intimate relationship" (O'Brien & Epstein, 1988).

The data significance showed the LVE improvement was 7.6% difference between the pre- and posttests for the mentees. Examples of journal entries included: "I feel very loved and supported; I also feel that I am very beautiful." The characteristic likeability is defined as "likable, popular, accepted by peers and included in their plans, enjoyable, companion, gets along well with others, popular in dating situations, expects to be liked, makes a good first impression" (O'Brien & Epstein, 1988).

The characteristic body appearance is defined as "physically attractive, pleased with appearance, feels that others are attracted because of appearance, feels sexually attractive, takes care to enhance physical appearance" (O'Brien & Epstein, 1988).

Body appearance showed improvement at 0.95% for the experimental group, indicating statistically significant differences between the pre- and posttests. One mentee stated, "I'm pleased with my body appearance. There isn't anything I would change about me in this area. It's my appearance that will get me noticed on many occasions." Another mentee mentioned, "My weight isn't where I would like it to be, but I'm extremely comfortable with my appearance. Just because I'm not at my ideal weight, that doesn't seem to change the amount of attention I receive from the opposite sex." The expectation that the control group results would not be statistically significant differences was met because they were not mentored in the mentoring intervention.

The characteristic body functioning is defined as "well-coordinated, agile, in good physical condition, comfortable with body, enjoys physical activities such as dancing or sports, feeling healthy and feels a sense of vitality and vigor in body functioning" (O'Brien & Epstein, 1988).

Body functioning showed improvement at 3.3%, indicating a statistically significant difference from the pre- and posttests for the experimental group. One mentee mentioned, "Staying in good physical shape and condition keeps my self-esteem intact. My self-esteem is at its best when I feel my body is at its best." The expectation that the control group would show no statistical significance because they were not mentored in the mentoring intervention was satisfied.

The characteristic personal power is defined as "powerful, successfully seeks positions of leadership, good at influencing others' opinions and behaviors, assertive, has strong impact on others" (O'Brien & Epstein, 1988).

Personal power showed an improvement of 3.82% that occurred within the experimental group between the pre- and posttests. The mentees' comments inferred that personal power was important. During the orientation portion of the intervention, one mentee asked, "What type of things would we be discussing?" The intervention was structured to be open and free to discuss whatever was of importance to the mentees. A few of the mentees felt relieved that they could be themselves and communicate on a more personal level. Throughout the intervention, several of the mentors discussed career and future plans, but the main focus was on personal goals.

5. **To what degree has maintaining self-esteem affected the self-esteem (MSEI) of Black women?**

Research question five is answered by analyzing the MSEI characteristics of self-control (SFC), moral self-approval (MOR), and defensive self-enhancement (DEF).

The characteristic self-control is defined as "self-discipline, preserving, good at setting and achieving goals, not easily distracted, in control of emotions, exercises restraint in eating, drinking, and/or the use of drugs" (O'Brien & Epstein, 1988).

The characteristic self-control showed an improvement of 6.74% for the experimental group between the pre- and posttests. One of the mentees mentioned that she felt that she was "off pace" for attaining her goals she had originally set, but she felt confident that she would eventually reach her goal. In observing the mentees, they seemed very self-determined to make their goals come true. Many of the mentees were college-educated, or about to enroll in college, and had already established the self-discipline it took to reach goals. Many of the mentees in the intervention share some commonalities in that they had strong religious beliefs and had positive role models as parents, close relatives or close friends. Because the control group was not mentored, there were no significant differences between the pre- and posttest.

The characteristic moral self-approval (MOR) is defined as "pleased with moral values and behavior, has clearly defined moral standards and acts in a way that is consistent with moral values, sets positive moral examples for others" (O'Brien & Epstein, 1988).

There were statistically significant differences that occurred within the experimental group between the pre- and posttests. The MOR characteristic showed an improvement of 6.59%. The mentees seemed to have clearly defined morals and beliefs that would lead them to set positive examples for others. Many of the mentees had earlier discussed giving back to the community by helping others. The mentees believed that having good positive role models, and being positive role models, were both keys to giving back and setting a good example. There were no statistically significant differences that occurred within the control group between the pre- and posttest, which supports the expected result of not participating in the mentoring intervention.

The characteristic defensive self-enhancement (DEF) is defined as "defensive, overly inflated view of self-worth, claims to possess highly unlikely positive qualities, denies ubiquitous human weakness" (O'Brien & Epstein, 1988).

There was a significant difference between the pre- and posttests in the experimental group for the defensive self-enhancement characteristic.

The defensive self-enhancement characteristic worsened by 4.12%. In understanding the defensive self-enhancement, confidence level or self-esteem of the mentees would have to be explored. The mentees all seemed to be extremely comfortable in their self-esteem levels before the mentoring intervention. Participating in the mentoring intervention, and working one on one with a mentor, may have supported the self-esteem of some of the mentees to the level of conceit and being overbearing. The mentors reassured the mentees of their perceptions and beliefs, and this could explain why the defensive self-enhancement was worse.

Satisfying the expectation that no significant differences would occur between the pre- and the posttest of the control group, there was no significant difference present.

There were four mentees in this group who showed no statistically significant differences in the characteristics. These participants were mentee numbers 5, 9, 10 and 11. Upon further investigation, some common characteristics were found among these mentees. All four of the mentees came from a background of strong religious support. These four mentees had strong female role models in their lives and, as a result, seemed amazingly comfortable with who they were and their self-esteem levels. All four mentees were single, and one had a child. Two of these mentees had college experience and/or an advanced degree, and one was about to start college. All four worked at least part-time or full-time, and one worked full-time while attending school. These four mentees appeared to have a strong foundation of support, which assisted in building their level of self-esteem, also increasing their ability to deal with life's issues. This could explain the lack of significant difference between the pre- and posttest among this group of four experimental group mentees.

There is a relationship between a mentoring intervention program and the self-esteem of Black women. The results were analyzed to determine the difference between the sample mean scores of both groups (experimental and control) for the posttests and determined that only the characteristic GSE showed significance. The difference between pre- and posttest scores for each group found that no significance was evident. The results analyzed the pretest scores to determine whether both groups had similar characteristics and found no significance was evident.

Key Findings

There were five research questions.

1. **To what degree will mentoring intervention affect the self-esteem (MSEI) of African American women?**

The findings showed that a statistical difference did occur between the pre- and posttest scores on the global self-esteem characteristics for the mentored group. The journal entries supported the findings of the mentoring intervention.

2. **To what degree has becoming aware of self-esteem affected the self-esteem (MSEI) of African American women?**

The pre- and posttests for the control group showed no change.

3. **To what degree has appreciating self-esteem affected the self-esteem (MSEI) of African American women?**

The pre- and posttests for the control group showed no change.

4. **To what degree will increasing worthiness affect the self-esteem of African American women?**

The pre- and posttests for the control groups showed no change. The experimental group showed statistical significance in all eleven characteristics of self-esteem. The findings for the competency characteristics showed significant difference occurred between the pre- and posttests for the experimental group. Journal entries were used to support the findings.

5. **To what degree will maintaining self-esteem affect the self-esteem of African American women?**

The findings for the lovability (LVE) and likeability (LKE) characteristics showed significant differences occurred between the pre- and posttests for the experimental group. Journal entries supported the statistical findings. The findings for the personal power (PWR) characteristic showed significant differences occurred between the pre- and posttests for the experimental group, as supported by questions asked during the orientation of the mentoring intervention.

Supported by input from the mentees, the findings for the self-control (SFC) characteristic showed significant differences between the pre- and posttests for the experimental group. The observational findings for the moral self-approval (MOR) characteristic showed significant differences between the pre- and posttests of the experimental group.

The findings for body appearance (BAP), body functioning (BFN) and identity integration (IDN) characteristics showed significant differences in the pre- and posttests of the experimental group. Journal entries were used to support the findings. The findings for the defensive self-enhancement (DEF) characteristic showed significant differences did occur between the pre- and posttests of the experimental group.

CHAPTER 5

Summary, Conclusions and Recommendations

———— ⟨◦⟩⋙⟨◦⟩ ————

A frican American women have limited opportunities to interact with other African American women in the workplace due to the lack of Black women in managerial positions (Duff, 1999). As a result, Black women often lack mentoring relationships with members of their race and gender. This study was designed to determine how mentoring programs impact self-esteem among Black women.

Methods

Forty research subjects and twenty mentors participated in this research study. The program participants were recruited through word of mouth, flyers and advertisements at community organizations and local businesses for five weeks. Once the program potential mentees were identified, the participants were randomly assigned to two groups: a control group and an experimental group. Group assignment was determined by random selection from a list gender. This study was designed to determine how mentoring programs impact self-esteem among Black women.

Many believe there is no relationship between mentoring intervention programs and the self-esteem of African American women. This intervention showed that there indeed was a significant relationship between a mentoring intervention program and the self-esteem of Black women.

The data was analyzed using The Multidimensional Self-Esteem Inventory (MSEI). This instrument analyzed and described the relationship among several variables (Locke, et al., 1998). Data was collected from interviews with mentors and mentees, observation, the journals that the participants used in the experimental group, and the data from the MSEI. The instrument measures the following eleven components:

Global self-esteem (GSE) as a measure of the highest level of self-evaluation; eight measures of the intermediate self-evaluative elements, which include: competence (CMP), lovability (LVE), likeability (LKE), self-control (SFC), personal power (PWR), moral self-approval (MOR), body appearance (BAP), body functioning (BFN), identity integration (IDN) as a measure of global self-concept, and the defensive self-enhancement (DEF), of all volunteers. The experimental group was exposed to the intervention and was matched with a mentor. The control group received no intervention.

At the beginning of the research project, all research subjects completed a pretest of the MSEI. At the end of the five-week intervention, both groups took a posttest MSEI. Pre- and posttest results were analyzed using the t-test, which is a comparison of mentoring and self-esteem, and an ANOVA test, which is a comparison that looked at the differences between mentoring and self-esteem. The degree of influence the intervention program had on the mentees was determined by the journal entries and interview comments made by the experimental group.

Limitations

This mentoring intervention was limited to race, sample size and sex. The research group consisted of African American women serving as both mentors and mentees. Sample size started with a total of forty participants: twenty participants in the experimental group, and twenty participants in the control group. Due to a variety of reasons, a total of five participants did not complete the study, four from the experimental group and one from the control group. The end sample size was 35.

It was necessary to limit the study to only African American women for both mentors and mentees to establish research that addressed specifically Black women. Future mentoring interventions should include more participants and cover a longer mentoring intervention period. The mentors would also be involved in future intervention to ensure the smooth transfer of information from the intervention and the contact sessions between the mentors and the mentees. These changes would enhance the research study.

Research Conclusions

To what degree did the mentoring program influence the self-esteem (MSEI)?

There was statistical significance in the difference between the posttests between the participants in the experimental group for global self-esteem (GSE). There was no significant difference that took place within the control group. The global self-esteem scale measures the subjects' overall feelings about self by asking about generalized feelings of positive self-worth and inadequacy" (O'Brien & Epstein, 1988).

The journal writing from the mentees shows that the overall mentoring experience was beneficial. The mentees had an understanding before the mentoring process of what they believed, but the intervention helped clarify some of their beliefs.

One participant wrote, "This mentoring intervention, as well as working with my mentor, helped me realize some things that I already knew to be true for me. But this experience added more support to this belief." Another participant agreed completely with the knowledge obtained. "I had been doing some of this in the past, but I didn't know this had a specific term attached to it. I'm not crazy after all." One final participant realized the importance of mentoring others through this mentoring process. "No one makes it alone. It's up to each one of us to make a difference in the lives of others."

The five-week intervention served as a Self-Esteem Enhancement Program. This five-week program is a group experience designed to increase understanding and awareness of self-esteem. Participants had the opportunity to assess their self-esteem, understand its basic components, and they learned how to work on self-esteem issues. They also created their own self-esteem improvement program and used group exercises to work on increasing self-esteem during the program and afterward.

The mentors spent time each week with the mentee reviewing the different topics of the intervention and sharing additional insight with the mentee from their point of view. This interaction gave more support and understanding of the topics covered in the intervention.

Through the use of mentoring intervention programs, mentors set high expectations of performance; offer challenging ideas; help build self-confidence; encourage professional behavior; offer friendship; confront negative behaviors and attitudes; listen to personal problems; teach by example; provide growth experiences; offer quotable quotes; explain how the organization works; coach their mentees; stand by their mentees in critical situations; offer wise counsel; encourage winning behaviors; trigger self-awareness; inspire their mentees; share critical knowledge; offer encouragement; and assist with mentees' careers (Shea, 1997).

To what degree has becoming aware of self-esteem influenced the self-esteem (MSEI)?

During week one of the mentoring intervention, the mentees became aware of causes of the increase and decrease of one's self-esteem and focused on the broad overview of the whole program of self-esteem. The mentees also learned ways to practice increasing self-esteem and how limiting those actions could cause their self-esteem to suffer. Becoming aware of exactly what self-esteem was helped the participants to influence or increase their self-esteem.

To what degree has appreciating self-esteem influenced the self-esteem (MSEI)?

Week two of the intervention addressed learning new ways to increase one's self-esteem and helped the mentees to appreciate the topic of self-esteem through personal achievements. It showed the mentees that they were valued and accepted. Identifying personal goals or dreams assisted in influencing the self-esteem of the mentees. The mentees also spent time understanding their MSEI results and where they rated among the eleven characteristics of self-esteem.

To what degree has increasing worthiness affected the self-esteem (MSEI)?

During week three of the mentoring intervention, the mentees were asked to write down ten positive features about themselves and share them with the group. This exercise showed the mentees they had positive traits that were worth mentioning and sharing with others. This experience helped the mentees to feel worthy of who they were.

Another exercise worked on enhancing worthiness by identifying common traps that could cause the mentees pain and heartache if they continued to dwell or exaggerate negative situations. This exercise helped the mentees limit negative situations and search for positive ones. Learning how to enhance or increase worthiness helped raise the level of self-esteem for the mentees.

To what degree has increasing competence affected self-esteem?

During week four of the mentoring intervention, the mentees focused on enhancing competence. Two exercises were used to problem solve and enhance competence. The mentees: (a) first realized that there was a problem, (b) stopped and then tried to understand it, (c) decided on a goal, (d) thought about possible solutions, (e) thought about their likely consequences, (f) chose the best or most realistic solution, (g) made a detailed plan to carry it out, and (h) practiced the plan. By increasing the awareness of competence, the mentees were able to problem solve, find better solutions and increase their competence and self-esteem levels.

To what degree has maintaining self-esteem affected the self-esteem (MSEI)?

Week five of the mentoring intervention focused on maintaining self-esteem. The mentees learned how to develop a self-esteem action plan, which worked on increasing and maintaining self-esteem. The plan identified a strength or a weakness to work on, then the mentees matched the issue with the four sources of self-esteem. The mentees identified realistic goals and developed specific and workable action steps to achieve their goals. After formulating these plans, the mentees were encouraged to practice them. This was the path to maintaining self-esteem among the mentees.

All eleven characteristics showed significance for the pre- and posttest scores for the experimental group. The definitions of the characteristics and the journal entries showed that there was a relationship between the data analysis results and what the participants wrote in their journals. The mentoring intervention also used exercises and discussion to gain better understanding and awareness among the mentees. None of the eleven characteristics were significant among the pre- and posttests of the control group. This result was expected because the control group did not receive the mentoring intervention.

This study concerned the self-esteem of Black women and the degree to which a mentoring intervention program affects the self-esteem of these Black women. Based on the research findings, the following conclusions are true:

1. Mentoring interventions affect the self-esteem (MSEI) of African American women.

2. Becoming aware of self-esteem affects the self-esteem (MSEI) of African American women.

3. Appreciating self-esteem affects the self-esteem (MSEI) of African American women.

4. Increasing worthiness affects the self-esteem (MSEI) of African American women.

5. Maintaining self-esteem affects the self-esteem (MSEI) of African American women.

Mentoring and mentoring intervention programs have an impact on global self-esteem, competence, lovability, likeability, moral self-approval, personal power, self-control, body appearance, body functioning, identity integration, and defensive self-enhancement of African American women.

Many have stated that there is *no* relationship between a mentoring intervention program and the self-esteem of African American women. The results showed that there was indeed a relationship between self-esteem and the mentoring intervention program. There was also a relationship between a mentoring intervention program and the self-esteem of Black women. The self-esteem of Black women in the experimental group showed an improvement between the pretest and the posttest scores of the experimental group.

Social Significance of the Study

This research study is significant in that it addresses some of the areas in which Black women have been overlooked or have been invisible in the past. This is the first known research study conducted for mentoring Black women, by Black women. It adds to the foundation of knowledge that addresses the importance of women-to-women mentoring and the view that Black women need each other to survive.

The Black mentors came from several professional disciplines and were able to build relationships with the mentees. The mentors encouraged professional behavior, taught by example, and inspired the mentees. The mentees were able to relate to their mentors and, as a result, learned from their insights and experience. The mentees used the mentors to help address some of their fears and concerns about their personal lives, expectations of organizational life, and insights on their careers. This mentoring intervention is not only significant to the Black women who took part in it, but it is important to all Black women as a whole.

Significance to Leadership

The significance to leadership for this study encompasses several factors, which include individuals, community, leaders mentoring leaders, mentoring programs, guidance, and a broader population. The individuals who participated in the mentoring intervention had an interest in finding out where their level of self-esteem started and where it finished over the five-week mentoring intervention period. This intervention was validated based on the fact that the self-esteem of the participants was enhanced as a result of taking part in this mentoring intervention. The individual felt empowered and felt that they had more to contribute to their environment and society in general. The individuals felt this mentoring intervention would help them make a difference in increasing their quality of life for themselves, their families, and their friends.

Community

Before the mentoring intervention, the mentees felt they had a voice, but they were reluctant to let it be heard. The mentoring intervention has empowered these individuals to let their voices be heard. The individuals were empowered to have an informed voice in making community decisions. The individuals can share this resource with members of the community. The individuals can help the community to develop trust, which is lacking in many communities and organizations.

Leaders Mentoring Leaders

Leaders could mentor other leaders and help them reach the levels of success that might not have been possible without them. Leaders mentoring leaders could keep young leaders from making career-limiting mistakes and guide them to look at career alternatives. Leaders mentoring leaders could increase the number of successful leaders throughout the organization versus having one or two for the total organization.

Mentoring Programs

Mentoring programs could be structured in an organization where a new employee is paired with a senior employee. The pair would communicate and gain a better understanding of the organizational needs, as well as the needs and expectations of the new employee. The senior employees could put the new employee at ease and develop a comfort level that would allow the new employee to have the confidence necessary to carry out the essential functions of their roles in the organization.

Guidance

Leaders as mentors could provide guidance and support to other leaders who could assist in retaining the new employee for a longer time. This could lessen the feelings of isolation that a new employee might be facing early in the process of entering a new organization. This could also build trust between the organization, its members, and the new employee.

Broader Population

As this study has shown, mentoring interventions have shown success among African American women. Although this mentoring intervention was limited to African American women, the information learned here would not be limited to just this group. Mentoring interventions could also be used to show success among other groups in the general population.

Recruiting programs by organizations could be structured to include Black women employees in the interviewing process to give interviewing Black women a comfort level as they consider joining the organization. This type of program could help organizations attract additional Black women employees. This could also show the prospective employees that the organization cares about their well-being and ability to succeed.

Mentoring allows Black women to experience a relationship that focuses on Black women's concerns and issues. This mentoring process created opportunities for African American women and opportunities for organizations. This information could assist organizations in retaining Black women longer. Through mentoring, African American women can break through the glass ceiling that tends to exist for them due to the lack of mentoring and guidance from other Black women. This could also bridge the gap between African American women obtaining leadership positions within an organization.

Implications

This mentoring process did affect the self-esteem of Black women significantly. Of the sixteen mentees in the mentoring intervention, eleven showed a significant increase in all eleven areas. This research study, like past studies, showed that women-to-women mentoring has positive effects. Black women share a common bond. This mentoring intervention suggests ways to raise the level of self-esteem in Black women that will guide them to become contributing adults in the workplace. The learning gained in the five weeks can be shared with others the mentees may interact with in their communities and workplaces. This mentoring intervention instilled techniques of self-esteem so that, over time, these skills become an innate process that will reside within these African American women throughout the rest of their lives. The community in which this five-week research study was conducted consists of .23% Black women. The study represents .00093% of this population (US Census, 2000). Although this seems like a small sample size based on the community, it's significant because it showed just how powerful mentoring is as it relates to increasing the level of self-esteem. It infers that the larger the group, the higher the increase in the self-esteem among the community.

The implications of the mentoring intervention reach well beyond the local community. Results from this study could assist organizations in attracting and retaining African American women. Based on the information that is supported by the data analysis in this research study, Black women learn from each other. Black women can mentor other Black women to ensure them that they belong. Mentoring lessens the feelings of being isolated in an organization when there is little, or no, representation by Black women. Building self-esteem through mentoring among African American women is the real concern of this study. This study, as well as others, has shown that mentoring brings about a positive effect as it relates to self-esteem.

This mentoring intervention program for Black women suggested ways to raise the level of self-esteem in African

American women that will guide them in becoming contributing adults. This program showed that mentoring does indeed increase self-esteem among Black mentees and can be used as a foundation for future research studies. This research study shows implications of organizational success, and the important element of this program is that the mentee can honestly say to themselves at the end of the day, "I am me, and I am okay."

This mentoring intervention has shown significance because, for the first time, Black women have information on mentoring and self-esteem that is about Black women, for Black women, who were being mentored by Black women. No more assumptions need to be made about Black women based on information read about in other groups. Black women no longer need to feel neglected or overlooked. Black women can now understand the process of mentoring and the affects it has on the self-esteem of Black women.

This mentoring intervention program showed significance because there was a need to understand Black women as a group and learn what is needed for Black women to grow and progress into successful leaders. Black women in leadership are so desperately needed in the community and the workplace. This information can help erase those stereotypes of Black women, so African American women can attain those positions of leadership that eluded them in the past. The voices of Black women can finally be heard.

My Declaration of Self-Esteem

I Am Me

In all the world, there is no one else exactly like me. There are persons who have some parts like me, but no one adds up exactly like me. Therefore, everything that comes out of me is authentically mine because I alone chose it. I own everything about me: my body, including everything it does; my mind, including all its thoughts and ideas; my eyes, including the images of all they behold; my feelings, whatever they may be: anger, joy, frustration, love, disappointment, excitement; my mouth, and all the words that come out of it: polite, sweet, or rough, correct or incorrect; my voice, loud or soft; and all my actions, whether they be to others or to myself.

I own fantasies, my dreams, my hopes, and my fears.

I own all my triumphs and successes, all my failures and mistakes. Because I own all of me, I can become intimately acquainted with me. By doing so, I can love me and be friendly with me in all my parts. I can then make it possible for all of me to work in my best interests.

I know there are aspects about myself that puzzle me, and other aspects that I do not know. But as long as I am friendly and loving to myself, I can courageously and hopefully look for the solution to the puzzles. I can look for ways to find out more about me.

However, I look and sound, whatever I say and do, and whatever I think and feel at a given moment in time is me. This is authentic and represents where I am at the moment in time. When I review later how I looked and sounded, what I said and did, and how I thought and felt, some parts may turn out to be unfitting. I can discard that which is unfitting, and keep that which proved fitting, and invent something new for that which I discarded.

I can see, hear, feel, think, say and do. I have the tools to survive, to be close to others, to be productive, and to make sense and order out of the world of people and things outside of me.

I own me, and therefore, I can engineer me.

I am me, and I am okay (Satir, 1988).

References

Allen, R. (2001). *The Concept of Self. A Study of Black Identity and Self-esteem*. Detroit, MI: Wayne State University Press.

Anderson, D. (1998). *Reclaiming the Power: Empowerment Strategies for African American Women in Higher Education*. Paper presented at the 11th Annual Nation Conference on Race and Ethnicity (NCORE) in Higher Education, May 28-31, Denver, CO.

Beale, F. (1979). Double Jeopardy: To Be Black and Female. In T. Cade (Ed.), *The Black Woman: An Anthropology* (p. 90-100). New York: New American Library.

Bell E.L. (1990). The Bicultural Life Experience of Career-Orientated Black Women. *Journal of Organizational Behavior*, 11, 459-477.

Bell, E.E., & Nkomo, S.M. (1999). Postcards from the
    Borderlands: Building a Career from the
    Outside/Within. *Journal of Career Development*, 26(1),
    69-84.

Bell, E.L., Denton, T.C., & Nkomo, S. (1993). Women of
    Color in Management: Towards an Inclusive Analysis.
    In E.A. Fagenson (Ed.), *Women in Management: Trends,
    Issues, and Challenges in Managerial Diversity* (p.105-
    130). New Park, CA: Sage Publications.

Bennis, W. (1988). *On Becoming a Leader*. Reading, Mass.:
    Addison-Wesley.

Bond M. A. (1997). The Multitextured Lives of Women of
    Color. *American Journal of Community Psychology*. Vol.
    25, No. 5, University of Massachusetts.

Braddock, J.H., & McPartland, J.M. (1987) How Minorities
    Continue to be Excluded from Equal Employment
    Opportunities: Research on Labor Market and
    Institutional Barriers. *Journal of Social Issues*, 43, 5-39.

Burke R.J. (1984). Mentors in Organizations. *Group
    Organization Studies*, 9, 353-372.

Burke, R.J., McKeen, C. (1989). Developing Formal
    Mentoring Programs in Organizations. *Business
    Quarterly*, 53(3), 76-79.

Burke, R.J., McKeen, C.A., & McKenna, C.S. (1990). Sex Differences and Cross-sex Effects on Mentoring: Some Preliminary Data. *Psychological Reports*, 67, 1011-1023.

Clawson, J.G., & Kram, K.E. (1984). Managing Cross-gender Mentoring. *Business Horizons* 27(3), 22-32.

Collins, P.H. (1987). *The Meaning of Motherhood in Black Culture and the Black Mother-daughter Relationships*. New York: Sage, 3,4-10.

Collins, P.H. (1990) *Black Feminist Thought*. Boston: Unwin Hyman.

Collins, P.H. (2000). *Black Feminist Thought: Knowledge, Consciousness, and the Politics of Empowerment*. New York: Routledge.

Cox, T.H., & Nkomo, S.M. (1991). A Race and Gender-group Analysis of the Early Career Experience of the MBA's. *Work and Occupations*, 18, 431-446.

Creswell, J.W. (2002). *Education Research: Planning, Conducting, and Evaluating Qualitative & Quantitative Research*. New Jersey: Merrill-Prentice-Hall Publications, Inc.

Crockenberg, S.B., & Soby, B.A (1989). Self-esteem and
    Teenage Pregnancy. In A.M. Mecca, N.J. Smelser, & J.
    Vasconcellos (Eds.), *The importance of self-esteem*
    (p.125-164). Berkeley: University of California Press.

Dalton, G., Thompson, P., & Price, R. (1977). The Four
    Stages of Professional Careers: A New Look at
    Performance by Professionals. *Organizational
    Dynamics*, 6(1), 19-42.

Davis, G., & Watson, G. (1982). *Black Life in Corporate
    America: Swimming in the Mainstream*. New York:
    Anchor Press/Doubleday.

Davis, M.W. (1982). *Contributions of Black Women to
    America* (Vol. 2) Columbia, SC: Kenday.

Deinard, C., & Friedman, R.A. (1991). Black Caucus
    Groups at Xerox Corporation. Harvard Business School
    Case No 9-491-047. Boston, MA: Harvard Business
    School.

Dubois, W.E.B (1903). *The Souls of Black Folk*. New York:
    The New American Library.

Duff, C. (1999) *Learning from Other Women. How to
    Benefit from the Knowledge, Wisdom, and Experience of
    Female Mentors*. New York: American Management
    Association.

Eased P. (1991). *Understanding Everyday Racism: An Interdisciplinary Theory*. Newborn Park, CA: Safe.

Faddis, B. (Program Director). (1988). *Hand in Hand: Mentoring Young Women*, Book 1, 2, and 3. Newton, MA: WEEA Publishing Center.

Fitt, L.W., & Newton, D.A. (1981). When the Mentor is a Man and the Protégé is a Woman. *Harvard Business Review*, 59(2), 56-60.

Fong, R., & Furuto, S.B. (2001). *Culturally Competent Practice: Skills, Interventions, and Evaluations*. Boston: Allyn & Bacon.

Gould, R. (1972). The Phases of Adult Life: A Study in Developmental Psychology. *The American Journal of Psychiatry*, 129,521-531.

Green, K., & Green, R. (1995, January). The Top 20-paid Women in Corporate America. *Working Woman*, 36-38.

Gutierrez, L. (1990). Working with Women of Color: An Empowerment Perspective. *Social Work*, 35,49-153.

Halcomb, R. (1980, February). Mentors and the Successful Woman. *Across the board*, 13-17.

Harris, D. (1995, January). 16th Annual Salary Survey 1995. *Working Women*, 25-27.

Hesselbein, F., Goldsmith, M., Beckhard, R. (1996). *Leader of the Future*. San Francisco: Josey-Bass Publishers.

Hill, L., & Kamprath, N. (1991). Beyond the Myth of the Perfect Mentor: Building a Network of Developmental Relationships. Harvard Business School Case No 9-491-096. Boston, MA: Harvard Business School.

Ibarra, H. (1993). Personal Networks of Women and Minorities in Management: A Conceptual Framework. *Academy of Management Review*, 18(1), 56-87.

Jacobi, M. (1991). Mentoring and Undergraduate Academic Success: A Literature Review. *Review of Education Research*, 61(4), and 505-532.

Komarovsky, M. (1985). *Women in College*. New York: Basic Books.

Kouzes, J.M., & Posner, B.Z. (2002). *Leadership the Challenge*. San Francisco, CA.: Jossey-Bass.

Kram, K.E. (1985, April). Improving the Mentoring Process. *Training and Development Journal*, 40-43.

Kram, K.E. (1985). *Mentoring at Work: Developmental Relationships in Organizational Life*, Glenview, IL: Scott, Foresman.

Kram, K.E., & Hall, D. (1989). Mentoring Alternatives: The
    Role of Peer Relationships in Career Development.
    Academy of Management Journal, 28,110-132.

Kram, K.E., & Isabella, I. (1985). Mentoring Alternatives:
    The Role of Peer Relationships in Career
    Development. *Academy of Management Journal*,
    28,110-132.

Levinson, D.J., Darrow, C.N., Klein, E.B. Levinson, M.A.,
    McKee, B. (1978). *Seasons of a Man's Life*. New York:
    Knopf.

Locke, L.F., Silverman, S.J., Spirduso, W.W. (1998). *Reading
    and Understanding Research*. California: Sage
    Publication Inc.

Missrian, A.K. (1982). *The Corporate Connection: Why
    Executive Women Need Mentors Treat the Top*.
    Englewood Cliffs, NJ: Prentice-Hall.

Mruk, C. (1995). *Self-esteem: Research Theory and Practice*.
    New York: Springer.

Mruk, C. (1999). *Self-esteem: Research Theory and Practice*.
    New York: Springer.

Murrell, A., Crosby, F., & Ely, R. (1999). *Mentoring
    Dilemmas-Developmental Relationships within
    Multicultural Organizations*. Mahwah, NJ: Lawrence
    Erlbaum Associates Publishers.

Nieva, V.F., & Gutek, B.A. (1981). *Women and Work*. New York: Praeger.

Nkomo, S.M. (1988). Race and Sex: The Forgotten Case of the Black Female Manager. In S. Rose & L. Larwood (Eds.), *Women Careers Pathways and Pitfalls* (pp.134-150). New York: Praeger.

Noe, R.A. (1986). Women and Mentoring: A review and research agenda. *Academy of Management Review*, 31(1), 65-78.

Noe, R.A. (1988). An Investigation of the Determinants of Successful Assigned Mentoring Relationships. *Personnel Psychology*, 41,457-479.

O'Brien, E.J., & Epstein, S. (1983). *The Multidimensional Self-esteem Inventory*. Odessa, FL: Psychological Assessment Resources.

O'Brien, E.J., & Epstein, S. (1988). *The Multidimensional Self-esteem Inventory*. Odessa, FL: Psychological Assessment Resources.

Ragins, B.R. (1989). Barriers of Mentoring: The Female Manager's Dilemma. *Human Relations*, 42(1), 1-22.

Roche, G.R. (1979). Much Ado About Mentors. *Harvard Business Review*, January-February, 14-28.

Satir. V. (1988). The New Peoplemaking. Science and Behavior Books, Inc. 28.

Scott, N.E. (1989). Difference in Mentor Relationship of Non-White and White Female Professionals and Organizational Mobility: A review of the literature. Psychology: *A Journal of Human Behavior* 26,23-26.

Shandley, T.C. (1989). The Use of Mentors for Leadership Development, *NASPA Journal*, 27 (1), 59-66.

Thomas, D.A. (1989). Mentoring and Irrationality: The Role of Racial Taboos. *Human Resource Management*, 28,279-290.

Thomas, D.A. (1990). The Impact of Race on Managers' Experiences of Developmental Relationships (mentoring and sponsorship): An intra-organizational study. *Journal of Organizational Behavior*, 11,479-494.

U.S. Bureau of the Census (2000), Department of Commerce, retrieved on June 15, 2003 from http:/www.census.gov.

Zey, M.G. (1984). *The Mentor Connection*. Homewood, IL. Dow Jones-Irwin.

About the Author

———— ❧❦❧ ————

Oftentimes throughout her career, there were times when Dr. Brenda J. Walker found herself being the only woman of color in a male-dominated and/or majority white organization. Walker knowns firsthand how it feels to be underappreciated and undervalued. As the only woman of color at the table many times, she found herself questioning her self-esteem, overall capabilities and her seat at the table altogether. After completing her dissertation project, she realized that it would reward her with more than a doctoral degree. It catapulted her into purpose and alignment. Today, with strategic focus, effort and time, Dr. Walker is on a mission to make a difference for Black professional women in all areas of their lives.

Passionate about continuous learning and giving back to the community, Dr. Walker seeks to help others navigate their professional journey, as well as the highway of life. After in-depth research and focus groups, Dr. Walker soon realized that much statistical data only showcased Black women as either a subset of all women or simply as part of the Black race. This gave her the ammunition and the gateway to create a movement centered around Black women as it relates to self-esteem through mentoring.

In her debut book, *In a Class of Their Own: The Power of Mentorship for African American Women in Leadership*, Dr. Walker highlights the barriers, the benefits and the breakthroughs of the mentor and mentee relationship. Through this literary masterpiece, she manages to weave together patches, like a quilt, which have been passed down from generation to generation. Exploring the unique patterns of each patch, Black women, like every patch within a quilt, has individual meaning—but speaks greater volumes when interwoven with others. Realizing that the "patch" of the African American woman has been overlooked in Corporate America for far too long, Dr. Walker seeks to inform and empower African American women in leadership to know and understand that the quilt of the marketplace is not complete without their "patch."

For booking and speaking engagements, email Dr. Walker at brendajeanninespeaks@gmail.com.

CPSIA information can be obtained
at www.ICGtesting.com
Printed in the USA
FSHW020652080521

9 781736 217078